The Significance of Christ in Our Lives

LEGACY of CHRIST

TABITHA HENTON LAMB

EBOOK ISBN: 978-969-4692-13-5
PAPERBACK ISBN: 978-969-4692-14-2

CONTENTS

INTRODUCTION

Let's face it. All of our problems began and will end in the garden as we can see in Genesis 3 and Revelation 22. The story of Adam and Eve ended with the promise of Jesus, our Savior, who would come from the woman's seed. But rebellion put a stake in the human heart from the beginning of man's days. Every seed of discord for humanity was sown in this early stage. To change the existing course and find answers to life, we must return to the scene in the garden.

Even if we had only the first three chapters of the Bible, they would be sufficient to show us the solution, for here the problem was both assessed and remedied. A solution was promised and provided before our first parents were banished from paradise. In it, we find man's purpose and identity.

God presents one compelling reason for our existence: companionship: "Let us make man in Our Image and Likeness. Let him have dominion over the lower realm of life, to have governance and dominion over all that We created." This is what He purposed in Genesis 1:26. All life forms are owned by God, the All-Sufficient One. He is complete in and of Himself, needing nothing and no one. His true purpose for humanity is defined here simply to share His life with us. What other reason could there be for our purpose?

We find God's initial assessment of Adam as he went about his task of naming the animals. He watched him as he called each animal, and observed that it was not good for him to be alone. This is the core purpose of humanity. Adam was already complete in essence and nature, but God put a counterpart in him and all of humanity, so that they could also enjoy fellowship with one another.

If only we could see it, we would know all that He desires for us is indeed what is the very best for us: complete security in Him. His plan for humanity and our individual lives is laid out here. He created us simply because He wanted us. If this were not the case, He could have abandoned us in the garden when we betrayed Him. But He did not: He came to our rescue. He stepped out of Eternity and clothed Himself in flesh and blood to live thirty-three years on this earth to carry out His redemptive plan for fallen man. He became the sacrificial lamb for man's rebellion and death, both in the spiritual and natural realm. He gave us the remedy to the dominance of three appetites —the lust of the eyes, the lust of the flesh, and the pride of life. And He saw to the ultimate defeat of the works of Satan to restore man to complete fellowship with Him.

And now I invite you to join me as we explore our legacy of faith in Christ through the following topics:

GETTING TO THAT PLACE

This chapter is all about my journey to belief. He met me in such a profound and defining way that I could discover the purpose of the tests and trials we face on our journey. I had to learn first to believe His promise that all the tests and trials are designed to deal with every intricate part of us that is not turned over to Jesus.

A KIND OF FIRST FRUITS

The Bible tells us that we have been crucified with Christ. How amazing! Before we were born, God cared for our future problems before they became our reality. Because we are alive in Him, Christ paved the way for a new kind of species—a new creation unto God. What is the cost of this new life?

THE SHROUDING OF THE FLESH

The shrouding of the flesh is our willingness to go through the process of dying to the flesh. What is the process and how can we come out victorious?

KINGDOM SERVICE

This is where the exchange of nature takes place to become more like Jesus through the ministry of the Holy Spirit. What training do we receive here to serve the Kingdom of God and no longer march to our own beat?

THE FOOL'S HEART

The Fool's Heart reveals the true hidden man in the heart of humanity. What are the characteristics of those who say there is no God or make Him irrelevant? How can we win them back to Christ?

THE PASSION OF CHRIST

This chapter provides a front-row seat to the total suffering of Christ through divine prophecy by the prophets David and Isaiah: the humiliation, the brokenness, the soul suffering.

The entire world was against Him as He carried its weight on His shoulders. You can see the battle of the will in the garden of Gethsemane, the battle of the mind and heart while He was on the cross. The question of why He had to suffer such an agonizing death is discussed.

GETTING TO THAT PLACE

This chapter is about my journey of faith as a young woman but, before we get there, I want to lay a solid foundation about faith. This is crucial if we want to walk in power and authority as sons of God.

THE POWER TO BELIEVE

Christ has authority over everything that moves. All things were made by Him and for Him—all powers, principalities, angels, thrones, even the law. On the other hand, the works of the flesh, sin, sorrow, sickness, and death came from the evil one. Father God has given Christ to be head over all things for His body the Church, and Christ has put all things under His feet.

And we who believe, have been given that same mighty power in Christ when He raised Him from the dead, and seated Him at His right hand in the heavenly places over all the demonic realm (Ephesians 1:19-23).

"If sin came from the evil one, how," you ask, "did sin enter the world?" Sin came into the world through the disobedience of one man, Adam, and that act of rebellion caused sin to spread to all men (Romans 5:12). You see, while God introduced the law through Moses—and the law was good in revealing sin and bringing conviction—but the law had its limitations. All it could do was condemn sin but it could not provide a remedy for sin. So, while we were aware we were sinning, we could not overcome our sinful tendencies. The curse of sin was to rule us until death (Romans 5:12; 8:3; 8:2; 8:4-5; 5:13; 6:6-21).

We desperately needed a Savior to save us from the curse of death. Christ was the answer. By exchanging His death for ours and by His resurrection, Christ defeated Satan and nullified his hold over us (Colossians 2:15–16). By doing this, He removed the law's ability to enforce the penalty of death over us—so now we can rejoice and say, "O, death, where is your sting? O, grave, where is your victory?" The sting of death is sin, and the strength of sin is in the law against us. But Christ

 Tabitha Henton Lamb

abolished both sin and death and took them entirely out of the way (I Corinthians 15:55-56). He made it possible for us to live above our sinful nature through faith in Him, and we can now come to God, who is a holy God, blameless.

So Jesus fulfilled all that was required in the law to make us accessible to God. Instead of sin and death, we now have a law of righteousness when we receive Christ as our Redeemer. With our old nature crucified, the body of sin has been put to death with Christ so that we no longer serve sin. Now, under the law of Christ we can continue in this new life, dead to sin and its hold over our passions. We can overcome our flesh when we yield our members as instruments of righteousness.

With the Holy Spirit as our Guide and Counselor, we can now understand grace. Grace is an expression of the love and mercy of God out of His good pleasure. It is not something we can qualify for or earn. It comes simply out of His benevolence towards us. Think of grace as the spontaneous gift of a loving generous Father to undeserving people, accessible to all even when we do not expect it. It's His divine favor, love, compassion, and desire for us to share His life all wrapped up in one.

GRACE TO BELIEVE

God's design for humanity includes the power to believe, and God has given to each of us a measure of faith (Romans 12:3). It is not something you can conjure up in your mind and drum up through sheer will power. No, it is God's Spirit communing with your human spirit. Christ's sacrifice has already made provision for all to partake of this rich inheritance. Jesus said, "In this world, you will have sorrow, but I have overcome the world." Sorrow is a result of the curse of sin upon humanity but Jesus overcame this sorrow with His sacrifice on the cross for our peace. He did not come to take our troubles away or take us out of the world, but as the Lamb, slain before the foundation of the world, He has provided what is needed for us to overcome it. You will still encounter sorrow, but He became the antidote to it.

Our new life in Christ comes laden with so many benefits but the main benefit is the gift of faith to believe God. In the garden, the enemy took it all. We were robbed by the devil of this in-built trusting nature when he sowed doubt and disobedience in our minds. So our trust turned to suspicion and mistrust of God. Because of sin, Adam was cursed with death because the wages of sin is death, spiritual death at first but eventually physical death. Sickness and disease are part of that curse. But the legacy of the second Adam, Jesus, is redemption for our sins and eternal life as our reward. Jesus declares to humanity, "Behold, I have set life and death before you and through My grace I have given you the power to choose"(Deuteronomy 20:19).

Jesus has not only freed us from curses, He has given us all authority and power to do miracles in His name (Mark 16:17-20). Great evangelists like Billy Graham, Kathryn Kuhlman, A. A. Allen, and numerous others have demonstrated His great power at work in us. I witnessed some of that power as a little girl at tent meetings. I did not understand how or why at the time. These evangelists operated in the power of the Holy Spirit, the source of power of God on Earth, bringing salvation to the penitent heart, the raising of the dead, physical healings and miracles—the blind to see, the dumb to speak, the deaf to hear—and casting out demons. All of this display God's desire for each one to come to a place of absolute faith in Him.

MY FAITH JOURNEY

My personal faith journey began in 2015, while I was going through a terrible divorce. I asked God if He would grant all of my reasonable requests in my divorce petition. If He would do this for me, I said I would give my whole life to Him. I would live for Him. I would put aside my disdain for ministry and the things I saw and experienced that made me question my faith. I would put all that aside and do His will for my life.

On November 20, 2015, as I sat in the courtroom, I listened in awe as the judge decreed the divorce. My petition was granted verbatim, exactly as I had asked. I knew from that episode that I had experienced an encounter with God. As I walked out of that courtroom with the evidence of what I asked for granted, I knew all stakes were now on me. He honored my request; I too must honor my pledge to Him. This reality was not a chore; I was so happy that He met me in such a precise way. I did not care what it cost me; I was resolved to repay it.

In my journey to seek God, my commitment was to consecrate myself to Him for one year. In the coming months, I received a series of words from the Lord concerning my grandfather, Frenchie. He told me, "The same covenant I made with Frenchie, I am making with you." I accepted it without knowing what this covenant meant or its details. By hindsight, I wished I had inquired about the covenant required, and the path I would take to get there. On July 24, 2017, He spoke to me, saying, "I have taken you and offered you up as Frenchie's seed." He visited me in a dream where He gave me all I needed to make the journey. On July 27, 2017, I received another word from the Lord. "You are Frenchie's seed. You will break ethnic, denominational, geographical, and financial barriers."

On March 22, 2017, in a dream, I had heard from Him the following: "You need to go to Blytheville, AR, to get something left behind that this family needs." I remember going to this place, which looked to be where my grandparents lived. On the way, I had to cross a park where I could see the back of the house. As I continued my journey to the backyard of the house, I saw a pond that separated me from the house. As I approached the pond, I noticed the bridge was broken, and parts of the wood were floating in the water. As I began to cross, I had to make my way on broken pieces. I noticed all kinds of fish of various colors, sizes, and kinds. My first thought was that these kinds of fish did not belong in such shallow waters. The fish would jump out of the water and circle me until I made it across.

I noticed what appeared to be a three-level home with a fence. I approached and knocked on the door, and a little girl opened it. I told her I was there to retrieve something left behind for my family, on the lower level of the house. She said, "Hang on," and went to get her mommy. When her mommy came to the door, I repeated why I was there. This lady was rude and would not allow me to enter even after I pleaded with her. I was desperate to retrieve the item, although I did not know what it was. She denied me the last time with a rude and hateful demeanor. But I stood right before her and told her, "All I want to do is to retrieve what my family needs, but you will not allow me." I proceeded into the house, and began to kick in doors. Some rooms housed bodies of people who were lying sedated and lethargic—like lifeless dolls stacked one on top of the other.

As I entered each room, I kept saying, "Jesus loves you. God is not evil; He loves you." Life returned to their inert bodies and faces. I heard them say, "You mean Jesus loves me?" I replied, "Yes, Jesus loves you." I went from room to room on all three levels. In one of the rooms a man was sitting on the floor. He had on a black shirt and a pair of jeans. He was holding a cell phone, and when I entered the room, He said, "You do not have to worry about anything. I've got you. Just do what you have to do." My thoughts were, "I've completely lost it!" As I went about my quest, the lady called my aunt and said, "You need to come and get Tabitha. She's over here tearing up my house and causing a ruckus. She is disrupting my house and you need to come and get her."

My aunt arrived while I was on the second floor. She called my dad and said, "Brother Alfred, this is not what they told me it was. It is outside my jurisdiction; you need to see this." By the time my father arrived, I was on the basement floor. Walking in, he noticed my aunt's disposition as she sat with her legs crossed reading a magazine. The lady proceeded to tell him what I was doing. And he said to her, "All I want to know is what did you do to her?" She didn't respond. However, I was in the basement. Consumed with preaching Jesus, I had completely forgotten what it was I had to retrieve from there. In 2018, I received a prophecy from a perfect stranger. She told me, "God sent you here (Louisiana); there is a place you must get to in the Spirit."

On July 28, 2023, I attended a family reunion. This family seemed unique, very loving, and kind-hearted. By the end of the weekend, I had all sorts of questions. I wanted to know more about their family, legacy, traditions, and identity. I discovered they had a weekly family prayer call, and I was invited to join them and co-host for a month. I said I had to pray about it, and I did. There was so much warfare behind this. Each week, I could hardly wait for the call to be over and the month to end so that I could separate myself from the spiritual warfare.

I asked the Lord again about the purpose of this call, and He responded, "Yes, this is for Me. I will use it." The theme He gave me for the month was "legacy." That word was burning in my heart. After the month ended around the second week of August, I began to understand the journey. While in prayer, I said to the Lord, "There is nothing I desire on this Earth. I ask You for just one thing: the gift of faith, the ability to believe in You." He spoke clearly to me, saying, "This is the covenant with Frenchie; it's the power to believe."

It was only five years later that I could fully understand the path I had taken. In the interim I had gone through unimaginable trials that no one would believe could happen to a woman. What kept me going was the strength that came from His words, "There is a place you must get to in the Spirit." I knew why I could never give up. I had to keep fighting at all costs. No matter what happened, nothing was worth me not getting to this place. God allowed each test, trial, hurt, and disappointment to take on a different meaning, and the approach to each had to be different for me to get to my destination. I had to fight for my heart and mind for all the right reasons, and not the wrong. I had to forgive offenses. I had to accept the ultimate in some areas of life that were absolute game-changers.

It was all designed to get me to the place to totally believe in God. Belief is the place He wanted me to get to in the Spirit. He spoke to me about it—absolute belief in Him.

The dream was in 2017, and the prophecy in 2018. It appeared my life went to hell and back after I received the prophecy, and I could not understand for the life of me how it was ever possible. All I knew was I had given myself entirely to God—at least as much as I knew how in my own strength. There were so many questions in my heart, but I knew it was not the time to seek answers. At the moment I had to survive with all my faculties intact. I had to be vital to exemplify God's overcoming power to my daughter, who looked to me as a tower of strength in tragedies.

During that reunion, I saw love; it caused me to seek to understand more about this family. It is what brought me to the covenant. I saw the covenant of God with this family, even though I could not explain what it was.

It was not until I petitioned God for the gift of faith—the power to believe in Him without question—that everything came together in perfect symmetry from 2015 up until today. The entire journey came alive in me. If I had to request one gift, it would be the gift of faith—the power to believe in Him, for this is the primary way to please Him. It is impossible without it. Faith is required in everything we do. He has given every individual a measure of faith. Through Jesus, He has secured all that is necessary for humanity to come to know

Him by grace and the ability to believe the new knowledge we gain from Him. For by faith, we know the Word of His power framed the worlds.

Before we are qualified to do the work of the ministry, our foundation must be sealed in Christ through the Holy Spirit of promise. The seal is intact as long as it is not tampered with through sin. Each of us will face our garden of temptation, just like Adam, Eve, and Jesus. There are only two options: to choose what the world offers to us at the bidding of Satan, or Eternal life through Jesus.

Now all the pieces of my life are coming together to form a picture. Everything intended for evil, God turned around for good to bring me to the end He has for me in this life. He taught me to record the journey, write about it, and put it in books. They are about the road I have traveled to believe in God. The ”Place” is to believe. It is a place in the Spirit. The trials are all designed to position us to believe in God—the only reason they are allowed. The outcome of each trial depends on our choice. Our brokenness is there to be healed and not to destroy us.

In the next chapter we will discuss what it means to be born again and how we can be like Jesus.

Reflections

Reflections

Reflections

Reflections

A KIND OF
FIRST FRUITS

The new birth is made possible with Jesus. It's a kind of first fruits of a radically different kind of life. Our first birth was in the natural but it was of the corruptible seed we inherited from Adam. Since what is corrupt has no power to redeem, the corruptible cannot save the immortal soul of man (1 Peter 1:23). However, our new birth is of incorruptible seed. It is of Jesus, the Word of God, who lives and abides forever. The Word cannot be separated from Him, for the Word is God.

> *In the beginning was the word, and the word*
> *was with God, and the word was God ... And*
> *the Word was made flesh, and dwelt among us,*
> *(and we beheld his glory, the glory as of the only*

begotten of the Father,) full of grace and truth (John 1:1; 14).

THE BORN AGAIN EXPERIENCE

So what is it to be born again?

That's the question Nicodemus asked when he came to Jesus by night. Though a Pharisee and member of the Sanhedrin, he was drawn to the teachings of Jesus and was fully assured that Christ was a genuine teacher of God. It was evident from the miracles of Jesus that God was with Him.

Jesus begins a discourse with Nicodemus concerning the need to be "born again" to enter the kingdom of heaven. One would suppose that a learned man like Nicodemus would have had both knowledge and an understanding of this principle. But this is something he had not met in all his books.

> *"Rabbi, we know that You are a teacher come from God; for no one can do these signs that You do unless God is with him."*
>
> *Jesus answered and said to him, "Most assuredly, I say to you, unless one is born again, he cannot see the kingdom of God."*

Nicodemus said to Him, "How can a man be born when he is old? Can he enter a second time into his mother's womb and be born?"

Jesus answered, Verily, verily, I say unto thee, Except a man be born of water and of the Spirit, he cannot enter into the kingdom of God. That which is born of the flesh is flesh; and that which is born of the Spirit is spirit" (John 3:3-6 NKJV).

Nicodemus understood birth from the natural perspective of childbirth; he assumed the new birth had to do with the will and nature of man. However, Jesus' message concerned adoption into the kingdom of God: to all who receive Him, He will give the power to become sons of God (John 1:12).

Jesus explained to him that what is born of the flesh can only be produced after its kind—flesh. A spiritual birth into this heavenly family requires the spiritual experience of being born again. To qualify for this new birth experience, "You must be born of water and the Spirit." He likens this experience to the phenomenon of the wind. You cannot see the wind, but you can feel it. Faith is required to accept the move of the wind of the Holy Spirit. So, it is with the Kingdom of God. It is an invisible kingdom established in the heart and unseen by the human eye. Faith in Jesus is required to see and to enter.

Nicodemus struggled to understand this principle because his carnal mind was still dominant. It was the state of my Christianity too. I was trying to take my old familiar self with its common ways of knowing and doing to grasp spiritual principles. Nicodemus took the scenic route of the carnal mind. He was looking to translate it into human terms to achieve it. He needed to bypass the carnal mind and its reasoning through faith and proceed straight to this spiritual truth.

It is why the supernatural work of God was not manifesting for me too—the way I needed to see Him in certain areas of my life. It is the same in our communities and society—the cause of our stagnant condition. I wanted to make His kingdom come alive after my kind, by the blood, what I could give birth to, by the flesh, with the five senses, by the will, what I could conjure in my strength. But that is not the way it operates. His gift is available to all who will receive Him. When we receive Him in spirit and in truth, He will give us the power to become like Him in our nature.

The religious leader must come the same way as the sinner. Nicodemus thought of a natural birth, but Jesus spoke of something greater: a new way of life, with new principles, a new heart, a new mind, with godly character in word and deed where we can adopt the nature and character of God.

So we were born again, not through the natural bloodline of Adam, or our cognitive ability, or our human will but through the will of God. Nothing in us would meet the requirements of a holy God or allow us to come to Him in and of ourselves. Our bent towards defilement cancels out any effort (Genesis 3:16; Galatians 3:16). That is why the sending of His Son was necessary. It was a perfect gift from the Father, not subject to change, variation, or inconsistency.

All truth is in Him, and He is the only One to epitomize trustworthiness. He will never turn away from us, even though we have the right to exercise our will to reject Him. He redeemed us according to His own will with the word of truth, which is that all men come to salvation. He is not willing that anyone should perish but that all should come to repentance. A longsuffering God is waiting patiently for all who belong to Him (James 1:18; 2 Peter 3:9).

We are born again only through God. And the WORD (God Himself) was made flesh, and He came and dwelled bodily among humanity. John says, we beheld His glory—the only begotten Son of Father God, full of grace and truth. He came bearing gifts of grace and truth. And He bestowed—not that we deserved it, but He promised it—sonship with the Father. What Jesus received from the Father, He confers on those who would receive in Him the right to be children of Almighty God, empowered to become a kind of first fruits. The Father loves us the same as He loves Jesus. The path is the act of simple submission, a simple path because no effort of our own is required. The provision is there, but we need to accept it. It's that simple, but it is we who make it complicated—creating a dilemma whether to believe or not to believe in Jesus (John 1:12-14).

SUBMISSION VERSUS INDEPENDENT WILL

Submission leads us into sonship of the Father. Sonship is the likeness of God versus the flesh with its carnality, the human heart with its corruption, the will in its utter rebellion, and the works of the devil. Our spiritual rebirth this time is not of the corruptible seed of Adam, the natural man, but of the incorruptible seed, the Word of God, which lives and abides forever. This Word of God gave new birth to you; it cannot degenerate to a state of corruption. It is perfect without the depravity of human nature (James 1:18).

What therefore are we entertaining that opens portals of darkness in our lives? For Jesus said *"the prince of this world cometh, and has nothing in me"* (John 14:30).

We cannot live without the Word and the Word must bring change in us. Temptation exposes us to the power of choosing against the will of God, that is, exercising our human will. This can go against us when we are immature and weak. Our bent towards evil enters when we try to enforce our will against God's will. It contaminates the heart of man just like it did with Satan, who was perfect from the day God created him until iniquity developed in him and caused evil to explode from within.

It is not until we no longer seek our independent path that we can give ourselves entirely to Him. We then willingly give up the right to fight, or defend our human efforts or desires just as He did not open His mouth to defend His rights or His life. When you choose to live like Jesus, you will model your life on the way He showed us. Even when you face persecution, you will be silent as a sheep led to the slaughter with no desire for retaliation.

When we truly surrender, what are we emptying the will of? We will see when we visit Jesus in the garden of Gethsemane. When He petitioned the Father to remove the cup from Him, you can at once see His human will surfacing. However, He overcame the power of the human will when He agonized in prayer with intense groaning until the soul and flesh were again brought in complete alignment to the will of God. He was now totally at peace with going to the Cross.

The key was trusting in the relationship with the Father. Oftentimes, we want the blessings of God without first seeking a genuine relationship with Him. As long as we receive good things with no sorrow, it is all hail King Jesus, but as soon as the test comes for character development towards maturity and growth, we are offended with God. We must learn to move past the satisfaction of our senses, and agonize in prayer to experience the blessed, sweet communion with Jesus in our suffering. Those who suffer with Him will reign with Him. We must take up our cross to follow Jesus. He fought His greatest battle in prayer until the soul and flesh regained their correct posture before God.

He petitioned God to deliver Him, but when the Father did not respond by word or deed, Jesus knew that He must conform to the Father's will. Nothing of His independent will mattered in this life-and-death crisis, only submission (Matthew 4:14; Luke 4:1-13). By yielding to the will of the Father, He had won the battle of wills before He ever went to the cross. And the cross was a necessity: it had to be endured. Redemption for humanity hinged on it. Dominion and authority lost by Adam hinged on the death of one in exchange for the life of many.

In this decision that came through testing, Jesus revealed the way to overcome our self-life and vain glory. He exemplified how to adopt a posture of surrendering our lives unto God, committed to the journey set out by a Holy God. The journey entails the shedding of the flesh with all its self-righteousness, self-centeredness, pride, worldly desires, pleasure, and works. It is the soul's fight for genuine righteousness through faith in a righteous God.

THE SHROUDING OF THE FLESH

I use the expression "the shrouding of the flesh" to convey the idea of covering ourselves with a burial cloth. This signifies death to our carnal self and its appetites. This shrouding and the removal of defilement come with abiding in His love and committing to love Him more. It comes in our continued obedience to His word. We receive salvation simply by believing, but we must grow in our belief through obedience to His word in our daily lives. As we grow, the proper question to ask is: what part of corruption remains in me? What doors to darkness do I keep opening in my life? For Ephesians 4:27 instructs us to give no place to the devil. He is to have no part of our lives, nothing in us to make us desire anything of this world.

Love for anything in this world is enmity toward God. We would then be actively opposing His commands and hostile toward Him in our pursuit of the lust of the eyes, the greedy longing of the mind, the lust of the flesh—its craving for sensual gratification—and the pride of life. All of these all have no place in our lives when we choose to abide in Christ. Now that we are born of the Word, the appeal of the things of the world should fade. Sin is of the devil, and having the love of this world shows that his desires still remain alive.

But Jesus came to remove our sins, and this is evident if we abide in Him and dwell in the secret place of the Most High God. We must remain in that place. We cannot visit or check in and out of it when it suits us. There is a world of sin that is governed and camouflaged for us by Satan. Jesus said that if we are born of God and remain in God, we cannot sin. In this, we show ourselves to be children of God.

We must abide until there is no need to exert the human will. It separates us from God, leaving us with no strength to resist this world's bewitchment, or our own depravity. Our only escape is to give ourselves entirely over to God, to lose the right to ourselves by submission to Him, to operate in survival mode that constitutes death or life until we lose the desire to resist, fight, or defend ourselves in the flesh.

Paul said we must bring our bodies under subjection to Christ. Is this not what Jesus did when He gave up the right to rebel, fight, or defend Himself? Was this not the reason the Son of God came into this world —to destroy the works of the devil. He came to mete judgment on the prince of this world and to cast him out. Having spoiled principalities and powers through the cross, Jesus made sport of Satan in an open show of his defeat, triumphing over him. Because of this victory, Father God gave all things over to Christ (John 12:31; Colossians 2:15; 1 John 3:8; John 15:2; 1 Corinthians 15:23).

So now we can reach for a higher order of life. However, we cannot afford to succumb to the enticements of the past. Jesus did this for all of humanity. Why would He suffer to entertain repetitive sin? We should not believe for one moment that the grace of God and the death of His Son was for such temporary purposes. The inexhaustible plan of redemption does not include a single measure of willful sin as a contingency plan. Let us not harbor such a belief. There is a severe warning in Hebrews 6:4-6 against falling away from the faith, and those who do, cannot be brought back to repentance because they would be "crucifying the Son of God" all over again.

Suppose it is true that we can go back to a sinful state, then why save at all? It is sin that gives way to death, both spiritual and physical, to sickness and disease, and to the enslavement of Satan. Why attempt a rescue plan if it did not encompass everything and was not all-inclusive? Why offer a partial benefit package? We must not imagine such untruths. If He is that God who holds all life forms together, who holds the earth continuously suspended in gravity, the One to whom the universe belongs. the One in whom all things consist by the working of the Word of His power, the One who sits outside of time and governs eternity, is He not powerful enough to deal with the rebellion of finite, created rebels?

Satan is a prince of a lower realm, a created being like us. If it were not so, his attempt to take over the universe in the eternal past would have been successful. He is simply not god over this universe and all of its life forms. Although he appears to be the god of this world with all its systems, this is as long as man's mind is given over to him through deception.

No, we are saved so as not to sin. The tests and trials that the believer must endure are the path God has chosen to take us to a higher plane of life in the Spirit, far above the realm of the senses. Where hurt and pain impact us, that is because our sense-life is so alive and kicking. But there is freedom where the Spirit dwells. I heard a preacher say, "The physical life is to be like a corpse. You can kick a corpse, spit on a corpse, slap a corpse, and it won't move. Why? Because it is dead." Dead is how we are to be with the flesh, subjecting it to only the role of vehicle for our Spirit and soul. *"And if Christ be in you, the body is dead because of sin, but the spirit is alive because of righteousness* "(Romans 8:10).

But, typically, we resist the molding and pruning of the character. It is uncomfortable and even brings great distress to the soul. What we encounter in the soul is not the same as what the spirit encounters. Here we exist in a stratum in God's realm, one that is above human reason and emotions, above earthly desires, above offense, above holding to past bondages, above revenge, jealousy, and envy, above reproach, above the tendency to exercise hateful or ungodly intentions, and above coveting. Character is its goal. The work and ministry of the Holy Spirit is to graft into us Christ's image, reflection, and nature. The choice is wholly up to us. If a seed falls into the ground and dies, although it abides alone it bears much fruit. We must let the mind of Christ reign in us. If there is a letting, there is a will. We shall reap the reward of a spiritual life here on earth if we are willing and obedient. He will never cast us out.

So how can we be of service to God? What does He require of us?

Reflections

Reflections

Reflections

Reflections

KINGDOM SERVICE

Just like the world, in the Kingdom of God we are evaluated according to the services we render. If we meet or exceed expectations, we receive a favorable end-of-year report with increases, promotions, and incentives for hard work.

The parable of the ten talents gives us a picture the kingdom of heaven's reward system. Each person was assessed and received promotion according to their performance. The one with the five talents immediately put his money to work with good stewardship and favorable earnings. He doubled the profits on the talents received. The same went for the one who received the two talents. However, the one who received one talent buried the talent showing total lack of stewardship, productivity, or earnings.

In due course, the master returned to settle accounts. In the evaluation, the one who received five talents and the one who received the two talents were judged to be faithful stewards of what they were in charge of. They met with approval and promotion. However, the one who hid the master's talent in the ground and returned the same talent, met with displeasure and rejection. What he had was taken away and given to the one who had the five talents (Matthew 25:14-30).

ALL FOR HIS GLORY

The parable teaches us that promotion in the kingdom of God is for service. We are to be good stewards of the talents He has given us, making full use of their intended purpose according to the design of the Giver of all good and perfect gifts. Our skills or giftings are not for personal fame or status but for service. If He can trust us with the little things He gives us, He will make us rulers over much. Our success is for His glory and His glory only; it defines the quality and quantity of our performance.

I remember while working for my last employer, there was a company-wide reduction in force (RIF). It meant selective termination at all levels of the organization, including the position of the employee health and safety manager. After some time, I informed my director of my experience in this area and he handed the duties over to me. Since the company now had two entities under one umbrella, I spent an entire year revamping and realigning the program with the parallel position.

When the time came for our company-wide safety audit, we landed a stellar rating of ninety-six percent, the highest ranking across the entire company. They did not post a picture of me all over the headlines. No, the company received credit for it. They took that stellar ranking to the shareholders, potential clients, and existing clients to maximize its highest potential. It was a great tool to grow their business. I could not get upset with them or demand they let the world know I was the one who achieved the stellar rating. It was their company, and they hired me to perform a particular job.

It is the same in the kingdom of heaven. We work hard, and are rewarded; however, we must give Him all the credit, glory and honor. After all, we are working in His kingdom, using His talents. God's acceptance of you does not make you a successful and profitable employee. No, true success in life comes from obedience to His instructions. And God values character. It is the purpose of humanity's redemption—to grow from children into sons. It's as important as the mission of sending His Son to redeem us. Now begins the work of empowerment to become like Him in essence. As the light of the world, He has called us to be this same light, the replica of who He is to the lost.

Even the world's employment system has protocols for ethical conduct and behavior. They teach you to be moral, have good character, and make sound judgments. Suppose you have gone through a new employee orientation process. According to your assigned job description, there are ethical procedures, standard operation procedures, and policies and procedures. Boundaries are in place to ensure you follow their rules of ethics and conduct, and there are consequences for violating the company's policies from warnings to demotion to termination of service, depending on the severity of the infraction.

While we are diligent in learning all this, many of us do not bother to know all of what we will need to be successful in the kingdom of heaven. Whatever rigorous training is required in a company, how much more in our Christian journey! We must stir ourselves to understand what is required of us, and, most importantly, understand the character of our Master, our new identity in Christ, and how to attain God-like character and conduct.

EQUIPPING FOR GROWTH

In addition, every new member should be willing to undergo training as we embark upon our new growth path. We cannot risk relying on the world's systems, ways, and methods to know the code of ethical conduct for Christian living and godly character. In the standard operating procedure to serve in this new kingdom, the role of the church is to make disciples for Christ. Extensive learning and training is required. And, just as Jesus Himself learned and grew strong in spirit, filled with wisdom and the grace of God, so must we also resolve to be equipped in our Christian journey.

We need to accept the fact that we have no power in ourselves because we are deficient in godliness. But God is merciful, gentle, and long-suffering, and rains His goodness on the just and the unjust alike. We are all beneficiaries of His love, care, and protection. The issue of trustworthiness tested Jesus in the wilderness, and so it is with us. Can we be trusted to do the job, accept responsibility, and be good stewards of our kingdom assignment? Without a complete renewal process, we open ourselves to danger when we lack character or integrity. Our character has to be established before He endows us with power with no exemptions to this principle. We cannot seek to possess the new with the old wineskins since our old corrupt nature, its habits and dealings intact have no capacity to embrace the nature of Christ. There must be a complete emptying of all ungodly characteristics, and then a filling of fruits of righteousness—to become the image and likeness of Jesus. What Adam did not pass down, Jesus came and revealed to us. He made it visible to the human eye, mind, and heart.

OBEDIENCE ABOVE WORKS

Sadly, some will miss the mark of heaven assuming their works are sufficient. But that's a fallacy. No good works will save us, it is only by obedience to His will for our lives.

> *Not everyone who sayeth unto me, Lord, Lord, shall enter into the kingdom of heaven; but he that doeth the will of my father which is in heaven. Many will say in that day, Lord, Lord, have we not prophesied in thy name? and in thy name cast out devils? And in thy name done many wonderful works? And then I will profess to them, I never knew you: depart from me, ye that work iniquity* (Matthew 7:21-23).

The one thing that causes us to deviate from kingdom business is sin. Sin breeds disobedience, disobedience breeds rebellion, and rebellion takes us on a journey through a place called process. What is this place? It's a place of correction to deal with that rebellion and sin. What is sin? Sin is transgression against the law of God. Our correction will bring us to recognize the lack of godly character in us and reveal the character traits He desires. This is so important because we need to be in a pliable, teachable mode in the hand of the potter at work. Such retraining is required to reshape the human character. Through it, we nourish our soul based on the word, and weed out all impurities that cause us to deviate from His will. We must reach the level of complete trust in Him, and His word above all else. That will determine the length of the training period ahead. Otherwise, we will go round in circles until He can call our attention to traits that are both harmful and invite the enemy to infiltrate our souls.

In the next chapter we will look at a category of people whom the Bible calls fools.

Reflections

 Tabitha Henton Lamb

Reflections

Reflections

Reflections

THE FOOL'S HEART

David begins Psalm 14 by remarking on how foolish it is not to believe in God. He describes this foolishness as the characteristic of one who disregards the word of God. This person is corrupt and left to the dreadful state of his human heart. The same is evident in the hearts of all who turn from Him. Let us be clear: humanity can do no good apart from God. Only a foolish person will hold on to the belief that there is no God.

In fact, God has protected humanity from its utterly vile nature when it tries to exist apart from Him. It is He who sets the boundary of the proud heart to conceal even our base nature from us and the point beyond which we can sin. He does this, not in a deceitful way, but in a protective way so as to save us from ourselves.

Jonah was a man who showed his disdain for preaching the gospel when God sent Him to Nineveh to cry out against her wickedness and to deliver them. *"And should not I spare Nineveh, that great city, wherein are more than sixscore thousand persons that cannot discern between their right hand and their left hand; and also much cattle?"* (Jonah 4:11). He protested In this, we can see the compassion of God toward the Ninevites and His desire to restore them to a state of knowing Him, which would cause them to turn from their wicked ways.

The fear of Him is to know Him. Is this not why the fool turns away from knowing Him—to avoid the conviction of his heart and thus continue to be enslaved by sin? Think about the widespread evil carried out by Satan all because of his rebellion against God. How much more for humanity, who are left to the wiles of Satan as their only influence? Is it not what we are experiencing in our daily lives? Are we not left to the hatefulness and corruption of our nature due to our willful disregard for the things of God?

The definition of a fool (Hebrew *nabal*) is "one who acts unwisely or imprudently; a silly person who is stupid, wicked, vile, impious, and lacking judgment or prudence" in his pursuit of independence from God and rejection of godly conviction. *"The fool hath said in his heart, There is no God. They are corrupt, they have done abominable works, there is none that doeth good* (Psalm 14:1). His vile acts are the result of the error of denying the existence or relevance of God.

And humanity responds in concert to this error. Perhaps the only difference between this world and Sodom and Gomorrah is the extent of their vile passions with no regard for the natural design of their bodies (Romans 1). We too in our pride in our technology and scientific minds, have disregarded any form of restraint in our ambition to become what we imagine. We need not look far to see the uniformity of the error of our ways. Our outward acts are enough to display the inward corruption of our true identity. With a seared conscience, our sensitivity to sin is too numbed to know the error of our pursuits. While we are not forgotten by God, it is we who have set ourselves completely apart from Him.

ATTRIBUTES OF GOD

How can we in our finite intelligence defy the awesomeness of the One who created us, and endowed us with so many gifts and talents? There is no fear of such a One perhaps because we have not taken the trouble to understand who it is that we are setting ourselves against. Let us therefore thoughtfully consider some of the chief characteristics of God: omnipresent, omniscient, omnipotent, immutable, holy and all-sufficient so we have the sense to pay Him the proper respect.

The omnipresence of God is "His ability to be everywhere and have an effect at the same time. The word "omnipresence" meaning "present everywhere" comes from the Latin roots, *omni*, meaning "all" and *praesens*, meaning "presence." "Omniscience" is "to have infinite awareness, understanding, and insight or to possess universal or complete knowledge." It comes from *scire* "to know." "Omnipotent," means "having unlimited or universal authority or force." It describes the state of an all-mighty deity. The word derives from the Latin *potens*, meaning "potent" or "powerful." "Immutable" means "not mutable, unchangeable, and unchanging through time: a fixed structure and properties whose values cannot be changed." "Holiness" is to be "morally and spiritually excellent, exalted and worthy of complete devotion as one perfect in goodness and righteousness; divine." God is also "All-sufficient," that is, "able to maintain Himself without outside aid." It refers to "the ability to supply His own needs without external assistance."

The person who gives up on God is under the same spirit as the one who chooses to convince himself there is no God. Both deny Him and their accountability to Him. When we abandon or renounce a religious or political belief or principle, this act is known as apostasy. For the Christian, it is denying God as well as rejecting in part or as a whole the fundamental tenets of our faith.

FOUR STAGES TO APOSTASY

Typically, there are four stages in the process of becoming apostate.

The first stage to denying God is when a person lacks the knowledge and proper understanding of God. He refuses to have a proper understanding of who God is in his effort to do away with God in his conscience, and to deny any conviction when he breaks His moral laws. It is easier to imagine He does not exist or is irrelevant in the affairs of humanity. How convenient to suppose there is no God or judge to whom he will ultimately be accountable for the error of his ways! At base he knows there is a God, but He wishes there were not.

In the second stage, a move towards depravity is set in motion. This is the natural outcome of rejecting God, or putting Him aside. The result of such a move is to live corruptly, do dreadful things, and intentionally live in ignorance about God. It follows that such a person forsakes prayer and communication with God, and stands as an enemy of God's people and an opponent of justice. It is the characteristic of the sinner that consciously pursues error. His thoughts and imaginations are continuously towards evil. Not that he never knew God. He did once, but he now chooses to forget God and to exalt corruption. Instead of using his imagination to contemplate and exalt God, such a man has allowed his heart to be consumed with only evil (Genesis 6:5).

Paul gives us a vivid picture of this lack of honor for God in the first chapter of Romans. He starts on the premise that God is made visible by all of creation, for all the universe displays His eternal power and Godhead.

> *For the invisible things of him from the creation of the world are clearly seen, being understood by the things that are made, even his eternal power and Godhead"* (Romans 1:20).

However, rather than acknowledge the Creator of the universe as Lord over all, such a person chooses to worship created things fashioned by man, and by implication make them gods. When he transfers worship that rightfully belongs to God to things made with hands, his heart has turned to idolatry. His worship is directed to man-made things rather than his Creator.

In the third stage, God finally leaves such people alone, and gives them over to their own debased minds. Although they knew Him, they fail to glorify Him according to their knowledge of Him. Ungrateful and futile in their imaginations, their hearts become darkened by their foolishness. Proclaiming themselves wise, they become fools. Therefore, God gives them over to uncleanness through the lust that is already in their hearts, to dishonor their bodies because they have changed the truth of God for a lie by worshiping and serving idols more than the Creator of all things (Romans 1:20-25).

By the time he reaches the fourth stage unrepentant sinners are already reaping the rewards of their error. Abandoning God's laws and formulating their own laws, they deviate from the normal course of nature, and God gives them over to vile affections and unnatural sexual appetites, both men and women.

> *For this reason God gave them up to vile passions. For even their women exchanged the natural use for what is against nature. Likewise also the men, leaving the natural use of the woman, burned in their lust for one another, men with men committing what is shameful, and receiving*

in themselves the penalty of their error which was due (Romans 1:26-27 NKJV).

Since they do not want to retain Him in their knowledge because of their obsession with their own pleasure, He gives them over to a reprobate, unprincipled mind. In the final stage of this apostasy, knowing full well the judgment of God that they are worthy of death, they dispense with any fear of judgment, and reach the height of depravity. Debased and without a moral compass, they lose all sense of judgment and ability to discern.

> *God gave them over to a debased mind, to do those things which are not fitting; being filled with all unrighteousness, sexual immorality, wickedness, covetousness, maliciousness; full of envy, murder, strife, deceit, evil-mindedness; they are whisperers, backbiters, haters of God, violent, proud, boasters, inventors of evil things, disobedient to parents, undiscerning, untrustworthy, unloving, unforgiving, unmerciful; who, knowing the righteous judgment of God, that those who practice such things are deserving of death, not only do the same but also approve of those who practice them* (Romans 1:28-32 NKJV).

 Tabitha Henton Lamb

The truth is man's fundamental infraction was against the glory of God. Man robbed God of His glory through his wanting self-reliance and pride. He is now in pursuit of "the glory of men." This deviates from his eternal longing—locked deep within the heart and soul—that only God can satisfy. The Glory of God encompasses who He is, all of His attributes visible for all to see, experience, and receive. Apart from sin, this quest for self-glory separates man from God. But Christ came to make Father God approachable to humanity being the express image of His Father. "*Whoever has seen me has seen the Father*" He said to Philip who requested to see the Father (John 14:9).

The glory is the array of His holiness manifested in His creatures, and in His redemptive plan for humanity. A time is set before us when His glory will fill the whole Earth. On our part that glory of God is reflected when we walk in total submission to Him. He is absolute in His holiness. The righteousness of God is the anchor of His glory. We are therefore responsible for upholding His glory, which is embodied and exalted in all of the Divine attributes of who He is.

Earlier we saw how sin came into the world through temptation. The motive of this sin is to be like God. That in itself portends the downfall of humanity. The pridefulness of humankind has caused such disdain for the manifested glory of God in nature and in us. In place of this, man has succumbed to the exaltation of himself as his ultimate goal. In this quest he draws upon his pride and all of the lust of the flesh, prohibiting submission at all costs, and making man enemies with God, a robber of the Divine glory of God in us.

This reminds me of a song by William McDowell *Falling on My Knees*, which goes,

> There are some things I can't see
> until I bow …
> I can see clearly now here on my knees
> I understand better here on my knees
> It is a beautiful song that should reflect the posture of humanity before God.

HIS GLORY WILL NOT BE CHALLENGED

Seeking the grandeur of ourselves is the height of our depravity. The peak of our pride is self-exaltation proclaimed from the inside out even to our destruction. That is the course many of us have chosen. While God ordained His glory to be reflected in humankind, man's rebellion left a massive hole in his soul that he attempted to satisfy with his vain glory. What an awful exchange we have engaged in, how utterly corrupt and against His intended purpose! The journey to our recovery is the shedding of the flesh, and coming to the end of all self-life and self-dependency. All of these are rooted in self-righteousness, self-centeredness, and pride. Each one contributes to the undermining of the human personality.

What is self-righteousness? It's convincing ourselves of being righteous in our own eyes, especially when compared to the actions and beliefs of others. That makes us narrow-minded, moralistic and sanctimonious. That attitude links us with self-centeredness, concerned solely with our own desires, needs, or interests as well as self-absorbed, self-infatuated, and self-interested. Self-absorbed people are only interested in themselves and their activities, and are intensely preoccupied with their own thoughts, desires, or needs. Self-reliance is the exercise of one's self sufficiency and resources rather than those of others.

All these are instigated by pride, which is an inordinate elevation of one's dignity. Our pride has utter contempt for the glory of God. For this, His righteousness must take vengeance in wrath, for He will not share His glory. And why should He with finite creatures like us? His glory is the justification for His righteousness. Our pride makes it impossible for us to submit to His glory. His righteousness must vindicate His glory through the atonement of Christ.

The definition of atonement is to make reparation for a wrong or injury. Christ paid for our wrongdoings when He repaired the infraction of our relationship with a Holy God. On the Cross, God chose to reconcile His glory with man's offense in his opposition to the glory of God. The Cross was the great battleground between God's righteousness and the pride of willful humanity. It is our only assurance against His well-deserved wrath. While the law reveals the state of fallen humanity, the Word secures our eternal redemption. Jesus, the Word, washes and cleanses the stain of sin upon the soul and flesh, giving us His Spirit to seal us. The law condemned us; His Word redeemed us.

We deserved His impending judgment against us—according to His righteous evaluation. Instead, He chose to set in motion our reconciliation through the atonement of His Son on the Cross. God set the parameters through faith for the demonstration of His righteousness to justify all who have faith in Jesus. Without the Cross, His righteousness would be vindicated in the judgment of the sinner to his destruction with eternal death apart from Him. Since His glory is as important as our redemption, He secured it by designing a way to both uphold His glory and to vindicate it. The Cross of Christ is the perfect sacrifice to repair the dishonor to His glory by our pride. Only the death of Christ could do it.

The Cross is therefore our witness against His judgment, the remedy to the pride of humanity. It puts an end to our self-reliance and our love affair with the praises of men. Born of the Word, it has the power to break pride in the contrite heart. It is the fair value exchange for what Jesus did. It crucifies self-reliance, self-centeredness, and pride in exchange for complete faith in Him as the foundation of our humility. That secures the glory of God in our hearts so that our dependency may rest in God and not in ourselves.

Reflections

 Tabitha Henton Lamb

Reflections

Reflections

Reflections

THE PASSION
OF CHRIST

In Genesis 3, after delivering judgment on Adam and Eve,
God gives a startling promise to Eve. It concerns the defeat of
Satan—the present ruler of the world—and the redemption
of humanity. God says He will put enmity between Satan and
the woman and between the seed of the woman and the seed
of Satan:

> *And I will put enmity between thee and the
> woman, and between thy seed and her seed; it
> shall bruise thy head, and thou shalt bruise his
> heel* (Genesis 3:15).

Who was this seed? It was Jesus, the Word made flesh,
born of a woman. He would perfect the work of redemption,

carrying the responsibility of sin and the wrath of God upon His shoulders.

> *But when the fullness of the time had come, God sent forth His Son, born of a woman, born under the law,* **to redeem those who were under the law, that we might receive the adoption as sons** (Galatians 4:4-5, emphasis added).

The bruising of the head of the one and the heel of the other foreshadow the Crucifixion.

> *Forasmuch then as the children are partakers of flesh and blood, He also Himself likewise took part of the same: that through death He might destroy him that had the power of death, that is, the devil* (Hebrews 2:14).

In this chapter I will attempt to capture the suffering Jesus endured to satisfy humanity's debt of sin and God's wrath for our trespasses. I will also deal with the question of why it was necessary for Jesus to die such a painful death on the cross and what are the consequences of such a sacrifice? We will be guided along the way by several passages, notably, Matthew 26, Psalm 16, Psalm 22, Isaiah 53, and Hebrews 5.

 Tabitha Henton Lamb

The gospel writers tell us that Jesus laid aside His majesty when He took on human form and dwelled among us. Now a mortal being, He had the same human limitations as us, governed by time, limited in mobility, and constrained to live within to the capacity of a human being. Like us, He became weary, and experienced emotional pain. There was nothing of the dignity about Him one would expect of a deity, no grandeur or splendor to draw people to Him. The prophet Isaiah describes His outward appearance in this way: "*he hath no form nor comeliness; and when we shall see him, there is no beauty that we should desire him*" (Isaiah 53:2).

Here was a man acquainted with sorrow who was despised by us:

> *He is despised and rejected of men; a man of sorrows, and acquainted with grief: and we hid as it were our faces from him; he was despised, and we esteemed him not* (Isaiah 53:3).

This was a selfless, meek and lowly Man, who did not identify with the high and mighty of society but with the downtrodden and lost. He offered healing and deliverance with compassion to all who came to Him for help. He spoke plainly, though sometimes in parables, unlike the erudite and eloquent speech of the religious leaders. But multitudes were drawn to

Him by the authority by which He spoke, by the miracles He performed, and by the care He showed. He practiced kingdom living by emphasizing love, compassion, and humility as the highest principles (Matthew 5), not the success principles of the world.

His godly character and constant reference to the Father reflected the perfect submission of a Son. For, though He was a Son, he learned obedience from what he suffered (Hebrews 5:5)—not that He was not already obedient; but this profound testing unto death perfected His human experience and showed us the way to perfection as well. Paul explains this:

> *For it became him, for whom are all things, and by whom are all things, in bringing many sons unto glory, to make the captain of their salvation perfect through sufferings* (Hebrews 2:10).

So Jesus modeled kingdom business, preaching, teaching, raising disciples and ministering healing and deliverance wherever He went. He was ever conscious of His Father's presence, and would after a hard day of ministry retreat to the mountain side to commune with the Father. Not only was He the way, the truth and the life to reach God but He showed how we should conduct our daily lives.

THE PASSION

Let us now trace the events leading to His death. This is a mingling of the historical facts with Bible prophecy concerning this pivotal event.

After the Passover supper, Jesus took His disciples to the garden of Gethsemane, leaving them to go further away to pray.

And he took with him Peter and the two sons of Zebedee, and began to be sorrowful, even unto death: tarry ye here, and watch with me. And He went a little further, and fell on His face, and prayed, saying, O My Father, if it be possible, let this cup pass from Me: nevertheless not as I will but as thou wilt.

And he cometh unto the disciples, and findeth them asleep, and saith unto Peter, What, could ye not watch with me one hour? Watch and pray, that ye enter not into temptation: the Spirit indeed is willing, but the flesh is weak.

He went away again the second time, and prayed, saying, O my Father, if this cup may not pass

away from me, except I drink it, thy will be done
(Matthew 26:36-42).

In the darkness, He was accosted by those who came to arrest Him, and asked "Whom do you seek?" He stepped forward and gave Himself over to His enemies while making sure His disciples were not touched. Even in His danger, He was concerned for their safety.

While the four gospels give a faithful account of the events surrounding His crucifixion, the prophets David and Isaiah received vivid revelation concerning the agony of Christ in striking detail one thousand and seven hundred years respectively before His time. We will use their words to tell His story of how He was esteemed, and yet stricken, smitten, and afflicted by God on that great and terrible day. Theirs is an accurate insider view of the heart and mind of Christ during His suffering, which includes His silent communication with His Father.

In Psalm 22, the prophet David revealed the anguish of soul as Jesus offered up prayers in His helpless condition. He went from bemoaning His state to comforting Himself in the Lord. It was a mixture of the outrage at the power and rage of His enemies and a plea for comfort due to anguish of His body, soul, and Spirit, longing for God to remain near to Him and not abandon Him. What were the afflictions of His soul? The first one was the fear of God's separation from Him, which overwhelmed Him with grief and terror. Yet He continued making His supplication to Him, crying out earnestly for His presence. Almost overcome by a sense of abandonment, He emptied His soul before God, declaring Himself forsaken by God, *"My God, my God, why hast thou forsaken me?"*as recorded in Matthew 27:45.

David heard those very same words as expressed in Psalm 22:

> *My God, my God, why hast thou forsaken me?*
> *why art thou so far from helping me, and from*
> *the words of my roaring? O my God, I cry in the*
> *day time, but thou hearest not; and in the night*
> *season, and am not silent* (Psalm 22:1-2).

In the psalm, Jesus likens Himself to a worm. *"But I am a worm, and no man; a reproach of men, and despised of the people"*(v. 6). It reminds me of the scarlet worm that oozes a stream of brilliant scarlet when put into hot water, an image of His blood.

Now He has been brought into the dust of death in absolute surrender with no way to defend His life from bloodthirsty men. Completely stripped naked, He looks down at His extended rib cage as He struggles for air:

> I am poured out like water,
>
> And all My bones are out of joint;
>
> My heart is like wax;
>
> It has melted within Me.
>
> My strength is dried up like a potsherd,
>
> I can count all My bones.
>
> They look and stare at Me (vv. 14-15, 17).

STRIKING DETAILS

Two remarkable details attest to the remarkable accuracy of David's prophecies. One is the casting of lots over His garments:

> They divide My garments among them,
> And for My clothing they cast lots (vv. 17, 18
> NKJV).

Compare this with the account in Matthew 27:35: *"And when they had crucified him, they divided his garments among them by casting lots."*

Then in Psalm 69:21 David sees them giving Him vinegar to drink when He was thirsty: *"They gave me also gall for my meat; and in my thirst they gave me vinegar to drink."*

Matthew 27:48 says: *"And straightway one of them ran, and took a spunge, and filled it with vinegar, and put it on a reed, and gave him to drink."*

Isaiah also gave details about His burial place: *"And he made his grave with the wicked, and with the rich in his death …"* (Isaiah 53:9).

The Sanhedrin had planned to throw the body of Jesus into a common open grave for criminals, but this was not to be according to God's plan. Joseph of Arimathea, a wealthy man and secret supporter of Jesus, intervened and obtained Pilate's permission to take Jesus' body and bury it in his own tomb.

STRONG EMOTIONS

Psalm 22 addresses the strong emotions Jesus felt. The first was the fear of separation from the Father. But even so, He trusted His Father as Holy and continued in praise to Him. He encourages Himself by dwelling on images of His Father's love and care for Him from young:

But You are He who took Me out of the womb;

You made Me trust while on My mother's

breasts.

I was cast upon You from birth.

From My mother's womb

You have been My God.

Be not far from Me,

For trouble is near;

For there is none to help (Psalm 22:9-11

NKJV).

And God was faithful throughout the course of His earthly life, protecting Him and taking care of Him in spite of dangers. Born in a lowly stable, sought out by Herod, His parents forced to flee with Him to Egypt, God's protection was always there. This assurance greatly encouraged Him in His deepest despair during His suffering on the cross. Prayer was His support. In agony, He prayed to God for strength. "Be near to Me, do not be far from Me." He was ever dependent on the Father to give Him courage, pleading to God to eventually deliver and rescue Him but for now to strengthen Him to fulfill His assignment to the end.

And as He suffers for the sake of His mission, our Redeemer assures Himself that God will deliver His soul from "the power of the grave" (Psalm 49:15) until He takes up His life again. He prays for deliverance from the all-consuming wrath of a righteous God: *"Deliver my soul from the sword, My darling from the power of the dog. Save me from the lion's mouth; Yea, from the horns of the wild-oxen thou hast answered me"* (Psalm 22:20-21). And He confidently trusts that His Father will deliver Him from the pit of hell in death, *"For thou wilt not leave my soul in hell; neither wilt thou suffer thine Holy One to see corruption"* (Psalm 16:10).

The second strong emotion Jesus experiences is the contempt and reproach of men. Though not as crushing as the withdrawal of the Father's love, it was grievous to His soul. Throughout His ministry on earth, He was criticized by the religious elite as an evil man, a blasphemer, a sabbath-breaker, a winebibber, a false prophet, an ally of Beelzebub the prince of devils, and an enemy of Caesar. These same leaders and Pharisees despised Him as a despicable person, not worthy of any recognition. He was ridiculed as a foolish man, one who deceived others and Himself. Those who saw Him hanging on the Cross laughed at Him to scorn. They proffered rude gestures, jeering at His nakedness and taunting Him who saved others to save Himself:

> *A reproach of men, and despised by the people.*
> *All those who see Me ridicule Me;*
> *They shoot out the lip, they shake the head,*

saying,

"He trusted in the LORD, let Him rescue Him;

Let Him deliver Him, since He delights in Him!"

(Psalm 22:6-8 NKJV)

But He took all that humiliation on Himself to compensate for the dishonor we brought to God by our sins. He submitted to the lowest form of disgrace voluntarily for the greater good of God and humanity.

We are all guilty for we have all sinned and fallen short of His glory. The whole of humanity is under the curse of sin and corruption. Each one is charged with transgressions. What is our transgression? We have all gone astray before our Maker, the One we belong to, each of us straying on to his own path.

All we like sheep have gone astray;

We have turned, every one, to his own way;

And the LORD has laid on Him the iniquity of

us all (Isaiah 53:6).

We are led as sheep to disaster. Some of us are ignorant of the rescue plan God has provided. Others sin willfully as a direct result of rebellion against God, drawing upon the hidden corruption of the human heart to reject His way for our own. Our sins bring upon us the sorrows in this world. Corruption is our soul's sickness and disease; our transgressions wound our souls. Our conscience, if not already numbed, suffers pain. Our grief and our sorrows are the penalty of sin.

THE ATONEMENT

But Christ undertook the responsibility of atoning for our sins to save us from the penalty we deserved. By the predetermined will and counsel of the Godhead, He was appointed as the One to restore honor to a just and holy God. Our sins were laid on Him for every nation and tongue, for every age and generation, when He was made a curse to redeem us from the curse of the law (Galatians 13:3). Since our transgressions were made against God, no one but God could remedy this. He did this by sacrificing His own Son. Justice demanded reciprocity and Jesus became the responsible party for our debt.

How do you justify it? What evil did He do? With nothing to His charge, He suffered as if there was a crime. What was His crime? He was accused of sedition against the state. However, He did not protest, not because He was not guilty but because they were simply human agents that were to perform the righteous requirement of God. Although no wrong was found in Him by Pilate, Caesar, and the Centurion, He uttered not a word to defend Himself.

He was oppressed and He was afflicted,

Yet He opened not His mouth;

He was led as a lamb to the slaughter,

And as a sheep before its shearers is silent,

So He opened not His mouth (Isaiah 53:4).

He is stripped naked. While Adam and Eve in their guilt became conscious of their nakedness, Jesus took the humiliation of being publicly exposed so that we may be clothed with a robe of righteousness.

His hands and feet are nailed to the cross and here He hangs for six hours in excruciating pain and anguish. The entire frame of His body succumbs to its weight of that hanging as He yields to the passage of death. He is drained of strength and His bones are dislocated—none broken but all out of joint by their continued stretching.

I am poured out like water, and all my bones are out of joint: my heart is like wax; it is melted in the midst of my bowels.

My strength is dried up like a potsherd; and my tongue cleaveth to my jaws; and thou hast brought me into the dust of death (Psalm 22:14-15).

No fight is left in Him. His mouth is dried up as His tongue cleaves to His jaws. His soul draws near to the dust of death. The judgment decreed upon Adam—"Unto dust shalt thou return"—is passed on to Him. The time has come for Satan to bruise the heel of Christ, the seed of the woman (Genesis 3:1-5); this is where the combat comes in. God did not deliver Him from the cup of suffering or from physical death. However, He did not allow Him to undergo corruption in His physical body.

> *For he hath not despised nor abhorred the afflic-*
> *tion of the afflicted; neither hath he hid his face*
> *from him; but when he cried unto him, he heard*
> (Psalm 22:24).

He was raised on the third day from the dust of death, resurrected that He might be the first fruits of a new kind of life.

WHY THE SLOW AGONIZING DEATH?

If the penalty for sin is death, one could wonder why Jesus was not given a quick death sentence to meet the just requirements of the law. Why was He put through such a slow agonizing death involving such physical and emotional torment? The answer can be found in Isaiah's account.

Surely He has borne our griefs

And carried our sorrows;

Yet we esteemed Him stricken,

Smitten by God, and afflicted.

But He was wounded for our transgressions,

He was]bruised for our iniquities;

The chastisement for our peace was upon Him,

And by His stripes we are healed ...

He poured out His soul unto death ... (Isaiah
53:4-5; 12 NKJV).

It is clear that He bore more than our sin. He gave His all
for us. The mention that His soul was poured out to death
suggests that every last drop of His being was spent in this
ordeal. It was to bear our griefs and sorrows; He suffered for
our healing.

The prophet goes on to explain why:

Yet it pleased the Lord *to bruise Him;*
He has put Him to grief.
When You make His soul an offering for sin,
He shall see His seed, He shall prolong His days,
And the pleasure of the Lord *shall prosper in His*
hand.

He shall see the labor of His soul, and be satis-
fied (vv. 10, 11).

I ask myself why did it please the Lord to afflict such pain
on the One He loved? Surely it must have pained Him just as
much in watching the punishment take its course. Yes, it did.
But the reason it pleased the Father was that it propitiated the
justifiable wrath of a righteous and holy God whose anger
knew no bounds. Sin leaves anger and deep emotional scars.
And when that anger was appeased, it provided the means
by which we could be totally restored in our soul. You see,
redemption made it possible to be legally restored but appeas-
ing the wrath of God opened the way for our emotional and
physical healing. That healing provided for the abundant life
Jesus promised in John 10:10.

It says here:

He shall see His seed, He shall prolong His days,
And the pleasure of the LORD shall prosper in
His hand.

But Jesus' life was cut short at the age of thirty-three in
the prime of life with no seed. Who then are His seed? It is us.
We are the seed of the labor of His soul and we shall prosper
because the Lord is well pleased with Him.

Consider the next few verses in Isaiah:

> *Therefore I will divide Him a portion with the great,*
>
> *And He shall divide the spoil with the strong,*
>
> *Because He poured out His soul unto death,*
>
> *And He was numbered with the transgressors,*
>
> *And He bore the sin of many,*
>
> *And made intercession for the transgressors*
> (Isaiah 53:12 NKJV).

We know that Jesus was numbered with the transgressors, the two thieves on either side of Him. But, symbolically, it meant all of us, for all have sinned. So He was cast among sinners. But even in that humbling state, He made intercession for the ones who caused His death, and that includes us. This means more than pray: it involved the pouring out of His substance for all of humankind, past, present and the generations to come. And for that selfless magnanimous act, look at the reward. It is the dividing of the spoil, or the sharing of the victory, with the strong. Who are the strong? It is we, the bold, courageous, redeemed of the Lord who have through grace become His sons! He did it all for us! Hallelujah!

The reward for His sorrows that overwhelmed Him as He met the wrath of Almighty God is ours to inherit because it says,

> *When You make His soul an offering for sin,*
> *He shall see His seed, He shall prolong His days,*
> *And the pleasure of the LORD shall prosper in His*
> *hand.*

We shall prosper and have fullness of joy—a beautiful example of the exceptional love of God toward humanity. Death is a destroyer of man's hope but when we receive the fullness of Christ, His death brings us into our eternal inheritance (Hebrews 9:15-17).

What man would go to such great lengths to offer complete restoration for us, the very ones who disdained His glory in pursuit of our own? How can the hardest of hearts not live with compassion and appreciation for Him? How can we not put our faith in Him? How can we not surrender and cast our crowns before Him in honor and reverential fear to love, adore, and praise Him? Who would deny submission to such a One who accomplished for us what we could not do for ourselves? All this was for the glory of God and to bring many sons to glory with the author and finisher of their faith (Hebrews 12:2).

HIS GODLY STANCE

All through this punishment, we see how Jesus maintained His inner purity by the truth of God. He brought the soul's suffering to the surface long enough to replace it with the comfort of God. He left no room for uncontrolled despair. The words expressing His pain were arrested immediately with words of faith. His belt of truth, His helmet of salvation, remained intact even in the throes of excruciating pain. His shield of faith continued to guard His faith in God. His gospel shoes were shod with peace as He forgave his enemies, and assured the repentant thief of paradise. His breastplate of righteousness was fastened on Him—not once giving in to sin. He forgave and interceded for those who crucified Him; He petitioned the Father to overlook their offenses towards Him and not count the charges against them.

As I close this study, I can see vividly how Christ would require all of the fruit of the Spirit to be flowing in our lives. If Jesus could show love and godly fear under such brutal circumstances, we too can operate in godly character aided by the Holy Spirit when we encounter our own trials. As Son and Suffering Servant of Father God, He showed impeccable character in all dimensions of spirit, soul, and body. Our hearts should bleed with repentance and compassion with a yearning to yield to

Him. We win or lose this battle called life in our character. Christ exemplified the nature and resolve we must take on during our tenure here on earth. We must love in deed and truth as secured in the love of Christ. We must learn to bind ourselves to Him as He did to Father God, totally dependent on Him regardless of the struggle or the need to protest our innocence during any form of persecution.

What a legacy to hand down throughout the generations! We are that legacy!

> *A seed shall serve him; it shall be accounted to the Lord for a generation.*
>
> *They shall come, and shall declare his righteousness unto a people that shall be born, that he hath done this* (Psalm 22:30-31).

Reflections

Reflections

Reflections

Reflections

NOTES

Dakes Annotated Reference Bible The Old and New Testament, with notes, Concordance and Index @ Copyright holders Melanie Dake, Edward Finnis Dake, Monique Germaine, Kimberly Dake Kennedy, Kathryn Dake Iglinksi and Dake Ministries Lawrenceville, Georgia KJV Edition @ Copyright 2014 Fifth Printing – December 2019

Matthew Henry Commentary on The Whole Bible – New Modern Edition Complete and Unabridged in six volumes Copyright @1991 by Hendrickson Publishers, Inc. Seventh Printing – January 2003

https://www.biblestudytools.com/commentaries/matthew-henry-complete

Merriam-Webster www.merriamwebster.com

https://www.dictionary.com

Wikipedia **The Free Encyclopedia** https://en.wikipedia.org

Oxford Languages | The Home of Language Data (oup.com)

The Supremacy of God in Preaching Copyright @ 1990 by Baker Books a division of Baker Book House Company, Seventh Printing – October 1996

Reaching the World with the Gospel of Jesus Christ – For we can do nothing against the truth, but for the truth. – 2 Corinthians 13:8 (wordpress.com)

Books by Tabitha Henton Lamb

The Spirit of Deception
How to Guard Against the Spirit of the Age

The ReCreated Woman
How to Incorporate God's Plan into Your Life

Contending For the Faith
The Battleground of the Mind

God's Plan For Man

Strengthening Your Faith
Toolkit For the Believer

The Surrendered Life
A Pearl of Immense Value

Weathering Life's Storms

Equipping Yourself to Face the Challenges

Understanding God's Plan

Re-evaluating Your Relationship With God

Understanding God's Plan

Re-evaluating Your Relationship With God

The Purpose of Pain

How God Uses Pain to Strengthen Your Resolve

Enriching the Immortal Soul

A Journey Towards God

Available wherever online books are sold.

Author Contact Information

You may contact the author at:

2008 Airline Drive, Ste. 300 #202

Bossier City, LA 71111

Email: admin@thlministries.org

www.thlministries.org

phone: 318-918-9248

www.ingramcontent.com/pod-product-compliance
Lightning Source LLC
Chambersburg PA
CBHW040152160726
48006CB00014B/1721